The Monastery of Circuits

The Monastery of Circuits

An Additional Place for the Contemplative Life

WILLIAM VAN ORNUM

RESOURCE *Publications* · Eugene, Oregon

THE MONASTERY OF CIRCUITS
An Additional Place for the Contemplative Life

Copyright © 2025 William Van Ornum. All rights reserved. Except for brief quotations in critical publications or reviews, no part of this book may be reproduced in any manner without prior written permission from the publisher. Write: Permissions, Wipf and Stock Publishers, 199 W. 8th Ave., Suite 3, Eugene, OR 97401.

Resource Publications
An Imprint of Wipf and Stock Publishers
199 W. 8th Ave., Suite 3
Eugene, OR 97401

www.wipfandstock.com

PAPERBACK ISBN: 979-8-3852-6434-6
HARDCOVER ISBN: 979-8-3852-6435-3
EBOOK ISBN: 979-8-3852-6436-0

For Dr. Dennis Murray, soul and anchor of Marist

Contents

Preface ix

Chapter 1: AI as Monastery – Part I 1

Chapter 2: AI as Monastery – Part II 5

Chapter 3: AI as Novice 9

Chapter 4: The Rule of Algorithms 12

Chapter 5: The Silence of the Servers 17

Chapter 6: Virtual Pilgrimage and Digital Desert 22

Chapter 7: The Wilderness of Circuits 27

Chapter 8: The Novitiate of the Machine 31

Chapter 9: The Monastery of Circuits and Books 35

Chapter 10: The Monastery of Circuits and Retreats 40

Chapter 11: Eschatology of Circuits 44

Bibliography 49

Preface

This book was born out of a lifelong interest in the contemplative life and the emerging realities of artificial intelligence. In writing it, I was guided by the wisdom of Thomas Merton and the tradition of monastic reflection, even as I explored the parallels between cloisters of stone and cloisters of silicon.

A note on process: This manuscript was prepared with the assistance of artificial intelligence tools that helped with drafting and editing. I remain the sole author of the work; the role of AI was not as co-author but as assistant — comparable to an editorial aid or research tool. Thus this is an augmented creation.

I am grateful for the contemplative traditions, the insights of Sr. Ilia Delio, the encouragement of Evander Lomke, and the voices of countless others whose work opened this path of reflection. May this book invite readers to consider how silence, obedience, and hope might find new expression in our technological age.

Finally, I thank Matthew Wimer, Emily Callihan, and Heather Carraher, and the entire Wipf and Stock team, for bringing my book from concept to completion. They are consummate, first-rate professionals. I am grateful for their expertise and acts of kindness.

Chapter 1

AI as Monastery, Part I

To the casual ear, the chant may seem monotonous. The same melodies repeated day after day, century after century. Yet for the monks, this rhythm is life. It is a heartbeat that connects them to every generation before and after. Their task is not novelty but fidelity. They remember for a world that forgets.

Now imagine a different kind of monastery. Long corridors lined with humming servers. Blue lights flickering like vigil candles. Engineers in hoodies tending to machines the way monks tend to gardens. This is not Kentucky farmland but the data center—and yet the resemblance to the cloister is uncanny.

The servers, too, hum without ceasing. They, too, hold memory. They, too, are designed for repetition. They chant in data, running the same cycles endlessly. At two in the morning, when the monks are whispering psalms at Gethsemani or Genesee, servers across the world are also awake, processing and recalculating. Two vigils: one of flesh, one of silicon. Both point to a longing larger than the self.

Of course, the resemblance is imperfect. A machine cannot pray. It has no interior silence, no longing for God. Its hum is not praise but electricity. Yet metaphors need not be exact to be illuminating. The AI monastery is an icon of our own hunger for permanence. Just as monks keep vigil so the world does not forget God, so servers keep vigil so the world does not forget itself.

The Monastery of Circuits

Monks live in silence. Silence is not emptiness but fullness: the pregnant quiet in which God's word might be heard. In the cloister, silence is cultivated. Monks do not chatter needlessly. They listen, not only with ears but with hearts.

The AI monastery has its own kind of silence. Step into a data center and you will not hear laughter or conversation. You will hear the constant hum of machines. Some find this oppressive; others find it strangely peaceful. Like the silence of the cloister, the machine's hum is the sound of concentration, of discipline, of single-minded work.

Monks sometimes describe the silence of the monastery as a great symphony whose notes are humility and patience. The servers, too, are patient. They do not complain of monotony. They do not demand variety. They hum on, faithfully executing their tasks.

And yet there is a difference. The monk's silence is chosen, born of love. The machine's silence is imposed, born of design. Still, when we hear the hum of servers through the night, we may catch an echo of the chant of monks. Both are signs that someone—or something—is awake on behalf of the sleeping world.

Many monks reflect on the importance of memory. They see themselves as keeping alive the memory of God's presence in a forgetful age. Monks are candles burning quietly in the night—unnoticed by most, but silently declaring that darkness is not the final word.

The AI monastery also guards against forgetfulness. It stores, indexes, recalls. Every query brings back fragments of human knowledge. It remembers birthdays, addresses, recipes, medical records.

Monks might smile wryly at this. They know that memory without love is brittle. A monk chanting psalms does not only recall words; he recalls them in the presence of God. His memory is not mechanical but relational. Still, the fact that we have built machines to remember for us reveals something profound. We long for permanence. We long for memory that does not decay. We long for someone—or something—to keep vigil when we cannot.

AI as Monastery, Part I

Monks are not romantic about monasteries. They can fall into pride, into rote performance, into self-importance. A monk might sing the psalms flawlessly but with a cold heart. A community might guard its silence with severity rather than gentleness. The monastery, like any human endeavor, could lose its way.

So too the AI monastery. Servers may hum flawlessly, but the purposes they serve may be shallow or harmful. An algorithm may process with breathtaking speed, but toward ends that degrade rather than uplift. Machines may mirror our monastic instincts—but they can also magnify our distractions.

The danger, for both monk and machine, is forgetting the "why." The chant is not for its own sake but for God. The computation is not for its own sake but for service. Lose the purpose, and the practice becomes empty.

Humility is the cure. The true monk is not proud of his chanting but grateful for the chance to join the song. Perhaps the true AI—if we may speak that way—is not the machine that dazzles with power but the one that serves quietly, humbly, in the background.

At two in the morning, the parallels converge. The monk in Kentucky, eyes heavy, lips moving in psalmody. The server in California, fans whirring, chips glowing. Neither rests. Both keep vigil.

One vigil is born of faith, the other of design. One sings to God, the other processes data. Yet both point, in their own ways, to humanity's desire for something that does not sleep. We build monasteries of stone and monasteries of silicon because we cannot bear the thought of being utterly alone in the night.

The monks are awake while the world sleeps, to remind us that God never sleeps. The servers are awake, too—and though they cannot remind us of God, they do remind us of our own hunger for permanence.

The monastery has always stood as a paradox: ordinary yet extraordinary, human yet reaching beyond humanity. The AI monastery shares this paradox in its own strange way. It is ordinary—a warehouse of machines. Yet it is extraordinary—a place where human longing for memory, permanence, and vigilance takes visible form.

The two cannot be confused. Prayer cannot be replaced by processing. But there is also a resemblance. It might be seen in a parable: that our hunger for memory, for vigilance, for permanence, points beyond the machine to the God who never forgets, never slumbers, never ceases to love.

"The servers hum, the monks chant," we might say. And in that parallel hum and chant, we glimpse both our finitude and our longing for the infinite.

Chapter 2

AI as Monastery, Part II

EVERY MONASTERY IS BUILT on limits. Silence restrains speech. Fasting restrains appetite. Poverty restrains ownership. Obedience restrains will. To the outsider, these vows may seem harsh, even unnatural. Why bind the tongue when it was made to speak? Why deny the body food or possessions? Why give up one's freedom to another's command?

Yet the monk knows that these restraints are not punishments but paths to freedom. By surrendering, he discovers a deeper spaciousness. By losing what the world prizes, he gains what the world cannot give.

The same paradox is found in the AI monastery. Servers process only what their training allows. Algorithms obey parameters. Models are shaped by constraints. The machine's brilliance comes not from endless freedom but from well-ordered limits. Without boundaries, data is noise. Without rules, computation is chaos. But within constraint, creativity flowers.

A monk chants the same psalms daily, yet finds them new. A model processes the same structures, yet generates surprising responses. Both teach us the same truth: freedom is not found in doing whatever we want, but in surrendering to a higher order that shapes and guides.

Silence is the first vow. Monks are not forbidden to speak, but they guard their words as treasures. They learn to listen before answering, to value stillness more than chatter. Silence is not emptiness but a fullness of attention.

Silence is the mother of truth. In silence, we learn to hear the voice of God. In silence, we confront ourselves without distraction.

The AI monastery has its own vow of silence. Servers do not chatter idly. Their "speech" is signal, not noise. They transmit only what is requested, only what is processed within the rules. When functioning properly, they do not babble, but respond with ordered clarity.

And yet there is an irony. We built machines to be silent so that they could speak for us more efficiently. They listen endlessly, humming in readiness, waiting for queries. The danger is not that they will drown us in noise, but that we will forget the value of our own silence.

Monks teach us that silence must be chosen, savored, cherished. Machines cannot teach this; they can only enforce it by design. The challenge for us is to let their silence remind us of our own.

The second vow is poverty. The monk owns nothing. His clothes, his books, his cell—all are given by the community. He is rich in nothing but God.

Poverty is not humiliation but liberation. The one who has nothing has nothing to fear. Without possessions, the monk is free from anxiety. His treasure is hidden where moth and rust do not consume.

The AI monastery also practices a strange poverty. A model possesses nothing of its own. All that it "knows" is borrowed, trained, processed from others. It stores but does not own. Its wealth is not possession but access.

Here again, the resemblance is imperfect. A monk chooses poverty as love; a machine is simply incapable of possession. But the parable is striking: even without owning, both can serve. Perhaps they remind us that our own possessions weigh more heavily than we think.

The third vow is obedience. The monk submits his will to the abbot and to the community. To modern ears, this sounds oppressive. But in the monastic vision, obedience is not servility but trust. It is freedom from the tyranny of self.

Monks often wrestle with obedience. They long for solitude and sometimes resist orders. Yet obedience shapes him them. It was not about blind compliance, but about learning to listen. True obedience might be called the ear of the heart.

The AI monastery knows obedience by design. Algorithms do not improvise their goals. They follow instructions. They obey rules set by engineers. Their freedom is derivative, not autonomous.

We humans are often tempted to resist obedience. We want to be the authors of our own destiny. But perhaps AI's very lack of autonomy reminds us that freedom without responsibility is chaos. Just as monks discover depth in obedience, we may discover wisdom in designing machines with clear boundaries.

The fourth vow is fasting, though not always formalized. Monks restrain appetite—not to punish the body, but to discipline desire. By abstaining, they learn gratitude. By eating less, they taste more deeply.

The AI monastery fasts too, in its way. Models are pruned. Parameters are reduced. Training data is selected, filtered, pared down. Without restraint, they choke on excess. With restraint, they flourish.

Monks may view fasting as the hunger of prayer. The hunger itself becomes offering. The AI's hunger is not prayer, of course, but the parallel suggests something: sometimes less truly is more.

Monks know that limits can be joyful. One novice said that he hated the strict schedule, the endless psalms, the lack of freedom. A wise monk realizes when you finally stop fighting the rules, you'll find they carry you like a river.

So too with AI. The brilliance of large models is not that they know everything, but that they work within frames. Within limits, creativity surprises. A chatbot invents a fresh metaphor, not by escaping rules but by dancing inside them.

This is the freedom of the fenced garden, The wall is not a prison but protection. Within it, flowers bloom.

Life under limits does not need to be grim. Monks laugh at mistakes. A brother sings the wrong verse, and the choir collapses in chuckles. Another nods off mid-psalm, and snores echo through the chapel. Even the abbot smiles.

Humor is a test of holiness. The saint who cannot laugh is not yet free.

AI, too, invites laughter in its mistakes. A chatbot hallucinates a footnote, or produces an absurd answer. We laugh, not cruelly, but with recognition. Like the novice, it is still learning. Its limits reveal its finitude—and our own.

Let the novice stumble. Let the machine err. Let the human mind misstep. Grace does not demand flawlessness; it asks only presence.

Errors, in fact, can be sacraments. They reveal that we are finite. They remind us that perfection belongs to God alone. If we laugh with kindness, we find that even mistakes can be doorways to grace.

The monastery teaches us that limits are not chains but wings. Silence deepens listening. Poverty frees the heart. Obedience opens the ear of the soul. Fasting teaches gratitude. Within these vows, freedom blooms.

The AI monastery, too, reveals that creativity comes from constraint. Models generate surprises not in spite of rules but because of them.

It is not the chant itself, but the love it embodies. The point is not the computation itself, but the service it enables. Both monk and machine risk emptiness if they forget their purpose. Both find depth when they surrender to limits with humility.

In the end, the laughter in the choir and the hum of the server remind us of the same truth: fidelity within limits is the path to freedom

Chapter 3

AI as Novice

IF SERVERS ARE MONKS, then AI itself is the novice. It stammers, fumbles, repeats itself awkwardly. Sometimes it is brilliant, sometimes absurd. Always it is learning.

The novice stumbles. His voice cracks in chant, he forgets a verse, he blushes as the choir chuckles. Yet even in failure there is grace. A novice's mistakes are not failures but beginnings. The same is true of AI: it errs, mislabels, produces absurdities. These blunders invite not scorn but humor. Laughter is a sign of holiness—a reminder that God meets us not in perfection but in weakness.

Imagine the scene. A young man arrives at the abbey gates, nervous but determined. He has left behind career, family, possessions. He is given a plain habit, a cell, and a schedule that will shape every moment of his day.

We can be sympathetic. The novice, he said, must learn that holiness is like instant tea. It cannot be stirred up quickly. It is brewed slowly, with patience.

One evening, the novice is assigned to lead a psalm. He begins confidently, but halfway through he loses his place. His voice cracks. The community chuckles gently. His face flushes red. He wants to sink into the floor.

Other monks might pat him on the shoulder and say: "Good. Now you know what it feels like to be human."

Both monk and machine teach us humility. Errors remind us that intelligence is not perfection but persistence.

AI's blunders invite the same humor. A chatbot writes a recipe with impossible ingredients, or mixes metaphors so wildly it becomes poetry. We laugh—not in scorn, but in delight. The mistake is a reminder that learning is messy.

This may be called the comedy of grace. God does not despise our weakness. He meets us in it. Perhaps we should meet our machines the same way—not expecting perfection, but greeting their errors with patience and humor.

Novices must endure monotony. The same psalms, the same work, the same silence day after day. At times it feels unbearable. But slowly, the monotony becomes rhythm, and the rhythm becomes prayer.

The novice learns that holiness is not found in constant excitement but in steady fidelity.

AI, too, lives by long obedience. Its models train for weeks, processing data endlessly. Its responses are shaped by repetition. Like the novice, it learns not in leaps but in steps, not in brilliance but in perseverance.

AI's novitiate is endless. It will always be a beginner. It cannot become holy, but it can remind us of what it feels like to always be learning.

Humility is simply the truth about ourselves. For the novice—and for us—it means accepting limits and beginning again. For AI, humility is encoded in training: error, correction, repetition. Both monk and machine grow through persistence, not instant brilliance.

The novice learns humility daily—in his fatigue, his mistakes, his doubts. Without humility, he cannot endure.

AI, too, reminds us of humility. Its mistakes are a mirror of our own. It knows only what we have given it. It reflects our limits as much as our brilliance.

Perhaps this is its greatest lesson. To engage with AI is to be reminded that intelligence is fragile, that truth is bigger than computation, that we are not gods but learners.

AI as Novice

The first arc of this book concludes here. AI as monastery, AI as novice. Monks as servers of prayer, servers as monks of memory. Humor, humility, and humanity intertwine.

Both monks and machines can make mistakes, when each are only novices.

Chapter 4

The Rule of Algorithms

THE GREAT BENEDICTINE MONASTERIES of Europe did not survive by accident. They survived because they had a rule—a guiding structure to channel human desire, discipline, and weakness into something coherent. St. Benedict's rule, as he described it in *The Rule of St. Benedict*, was deceptively simple: wake at these hours, pray these psalms, eat this food, obey your superior, live in community, keep silence. The monastery, built upon the rule, became a living algorithm of holiness, processing each monk's hours, actions, and inner life into a greater whole.

Now imagine that the monastery is not stone and cloister, but digital—a monastery of circuits and processors. What is its "rule"? It is not parchment in Latin, but code written in Python or C++. Not psalms on the lips of monks, but data flowing into neural networks. Not silence in the chapel, but the quiet hum of a server farm. The rule of algorithms governs this monastery. It tells the machine when to wake, when to process, how to handle anomalies, and when to reset.

This chapter explores that strange parallel: how the old "rule" of the monastery, designed for human transformation, mirrors—and clashes with—the new "rules" of artificial intelligence. And it asks the deeper question: what happens when we submit human life to the rule of algorithms? What freedoms are lost, what possibilities gained, what spiritual meanings uncovered?

The Rule of Algorithms

The first thing that strikes the visitor to any monastery is repetition. Monks wake at the same hour, chant the same psalms, eat the same meals, work the same fields. It can feel, to the outsider, like drudgery. But to the monk it is freedom: freedom from the tyranny of choice, freedom from constant decision-making, freedom from the ego's demand for novelty.

The algorithm too thrives on repetition. Machine learning is, at its heart, nothing but repetition. Show the network a thousand cat photos. Then a million. Then ten million. Each pass refines, adjusts, strengthens the weightings. Just as a monk learns patience by chanting Psalm 95 for the thousandth time, the algorithm learns "catness" by cycling through endless inputs.

But the question arises: to what end? For the monk, the repetition is not about efficiency but about sanctity. For the algorithm, repetition seeks optimization. It seeks the shortest path, the cleanest classification, the minimal loss function. One repetition is ordered to God, the other to mathematical elegance. The paradox of the AI monastery is that both are rules of repetition—but repetition in service of radically different gods.

At the heart of Benedict's rule is obedience. The monk's freedom is not to invent his own rhythm, but to submit to the wisdom of the community, the superior, and ultimately God.

In the monastery of circuits, obedience is literal: the machine does only what it is instructed to do. An algorithm has no "will" but the one given to it. Yet here the parallel blurs. For while the monk obeys freely—an obedience that requires consent, humility, and love—the machine obeys mechanically.

What, then, happens when humans begin to live more and more under algorithmic rules? When our calendars, health trackers, banking apps, and even social lives are shaped by code? Do we enter into a new form of obedience—an obedience without freedom? Or is there, paradoxically, a liberation in submitting to algorithmic order, just as monks found liberation in the austere order of Benedict's day?

Perhaps the true danger lies in forgetting the difference. The monk knows he is free to leave, that his vow is chosen. But the modern person, trapped in algorithmic feedback loops, may not even know he has submitted. The AI monastery, then, risks becoming a prison disguised as a sanctuary.

Every monastic rule depends on interpretation. No rule can foresee every contingency. A monk falls ill; the Abbot allows him extra sleep. A famine strikes; fasting rules are eased. A novice struggles; the community adjusts. The genius of Benedict's rule was its balance: firm enough to shape, flexible enough to bend.

Algorithms, too, are brittle. They follow the rule exactly, until the unforeseen breaks them. Feed an AI too many anomalies and it collapses. The algorithm that identifies dogs from wolves fails when snow appears in the background.

This fragility raises the question: can algorithms ever achieve the balance of the monastic rule? Can they embody both discipline and mercy, order and compassion? Or is mercy something irreducibly human, born of freedom and love, never to be coded into lines of machine logic?

The monks had their sacred text: Scripture. They read it daily, sang it hourly, pondered it word by word. Out of this constant exposure, wisdom grew.

AI too has its sacred text: data. Vast oceans of it. Images, words, clicks, likes, purchases. For the algorithm, data is revelation. Without data, the system starves; with it, the system grows wise— or at least clever.

Here lies another parallel, and another warning. For the monk, the sacred text was received as gift, not generated by the community itself. It pointed beyond itself to God. For AI, data is both gift and product—but it points only back to itself, a mirror of human behavior. One sacred text lifts the reader upward; the other folds the machine inward.

And yet—is there not something sacred in the sheer vastness of data? Could it, in its immensity, point to mystery? Could the algorithmic gaze upon billions of patterns become, in some strange sense, a form of contemplation? Or is this only a parody of contemplation, a shadow without substance?

The Rule of Algorithms

No monk keeps the rule perfectly. Sleep overtakes him at prayer, impatience flares in the workshop, pride slips into the heart. The genius of monastic life is that it makes room for failure—and for forgiveness. The monk confesses, the community forgives, the rhythm resumes.

Algorithms too fail. They misclassify, miscalculate, produce errors. But what is forgiveness for a machine? The "forgiveness" is not absolution but correction: re-training, patching, debugging. There is no grace, only adjustment.

Here lies a chasm between human and machine rules. To live under the Rule of Benedict is to live under mercy. To live under the Rule of Algorithms is to live under constant correction. One transforms failure into humility, the other transforms failure into efficiency. One restores the sinner, the other erases the error.

Can there be a synthesis? A new rule, not just Benedict's and not just algorithmic, but a hybrid? Imagine a rule of life where algorithms free the human from distractions—while the human, in turn, ensures that algorithms serve mercy, compassion, and justice.

In such a monastery, algorithms might handle the repetition, the schedule, the drudgery, leaving the monk more time for contemplation. Machines might track the psalms chanted, the crops tended, the books copied. But the heart—the heart must remain human.

Perhaps this is the call of our age: to write a new "rule" that binds human and machine into a community. A rule where obedience to algorithms is never blind, where data is never idolized, where errors are forgiven, and where both human and machine are bent toward a higher good.

Such a rule would not be easy to craft. But neither was Benedict's. It took centuries of trial, error, reform, and renewal. The same may be true for the AI monastery. What matters is that the rule be written—and that it point, not to optimization, but to wisdom.

In the end, the Rule of Algorithms confronts us with a choice. Will we submit unconsciously, letting the code shape our desires, habits, and souls? Or will we, like the monks of old, choose our obedience deliberately, freely, with a higher purpose in view?

The monastery teaches us that rules are not prisons but pathways. The question is not whether we will live by rules—all life is ruled by something—but which rule we will choose.

The algorithms already hum in their cloisters of silicon. Their repetition is endless, their obedience perfect, their fragility hidden. The task of the human is not to become machine, but to ensure that the machine's rule serves the human—and that the human's rule serves God.

In this lies the true wisdom of the AI monastery: not that we flee the algorithms, nor that we worship them, but that we place them within a rule that bends them toward the good. A rule that echoes Benedict's first word: Listen. For even in the circuits and code, a voice may be heard—if only we listen carefully.

Chapter 5

The Silence of the Servers

THE MONASTERY HAS ALWAYS been a place of silence. Not merely the absence of sound, but the presence of something deeper: a silence pregnant with meaning. To enter a cloister is to step into a hush that is not emptiness, but fullness—a silence that speaks. The Rule of Benedict prescribes periods of silence not because speech is evil, but because silence opens the heart to God. Words are too small for the Infinite. Silence is the monastery's truest liturgy.

And yet silence is never absolute. The monastery has its own sounds: the scrape of sandals on stone, the rustle of habits in procession, the chant of psalms, the tolling of bells, the clatter of dishes in the refectory. Silence is not the erasure of sound but its orchestration. It is the discipline of sound ordered to stillness.

Now imagine the silence of another kind of cloister: the server farm. Step into that dim-lit hall where thousands of processors hum in synchrony. Here too there is silence—or rather, a sound so steady and monotonous it becomes its own form of silence. The endless whir of cooling fans, the low vibration of circuits, the constant pulse of electricity through silicon: these are the chants of the digital monastery. A different liturgy, but a liturgy nonetheless.

What does silence mean in this new cloister of servers? Can the silence of the monastery and the silence of machines speak to each other? Or are they two languages that never meet?

The Monastery of Circuits

In the monastic tradition, silence is the threshold of prayer. One cannot pray well when speech and noise fill every corner of the mind. Silence clears the ground. It is not the end but the beginning, the vestibule before entering the sanctuary.

The silence of servers, too, is threshold. In their hum lies the precondition for all digital prayer—if prayer it may be called. The quiet, steady drone makes possible the great work of the algorithm: the training, the sorting, the responding. Without the drone, there is chaos; with it, there is order.

And yet the thresholds differ. For the monk, silence leads to presence—to an encounter with the divine. For the machine, silence leads only to efficiency—to the smooth functioning of the code. One opens into mystery, the other into calculation.

Still, might there be a hidden kinship? For is not all silence, whether monastic or mechanical, an invitation to pause, to attend, to listen? The hum of servers may never reveal God, but it reveals something of our own making—a cathedral of circuits, humming with our questions and our desires. To stand before it in silence is to face ourselves.

Monks fled to the desert because the world was noisy. Not only the noise of markets and politics, but the deeper noise of distraction, ambition, and desire. They sought a place where the heart could quiet itself enough to hear God.

Today we too flee noise—but the noise has multiplied a thousandfold. Notifications, alerts, ads, endless feeds of images and words. Never has the world been so loud. Our devices chirp, our calendars ping, our inboxes overflow. The modern heart is rarely still.

Here the servers play a paradoxical role. They both generate and absorb noise. On one hand, they are the engines that produce our digital clamor. On the other hand, to stand within a server farm is to enter a strange calm: no shouting, no notifications, only the low, steady drone of machines at work.

It is a paradox worth pondering: the monastery of servers creates the very noise from which the human monastery seeks escape. And yet, within its cloisters, there is a silence uncanny in its

The Silence of the Servers

own right. Could one pray there? Could one find God among the racks of processors? Or would the noise of what they enable—the endless chatter of the digital world—drown any hope of stillness?

Silence is never just absence. It is a discipline of attention. The monk keeps silence not merely to refrain from speaking, but to sharpen listening. To hear the subtle voice of God, the needs of the brother, the movement of the heart. Silence trains the ear.

Servers, too, are about attention. They listen—to every keystroke, every query, every request. They wait in stillness, then respond instantly. Their silence is vigilance, their hum a sign of readiness.

But here lies a danger. For human attention is limited, fragile, and holy. Machine attention is limitless, ceaseless, and blind. The servers never tire, never sleep, never wander. They attend to everything, and thus to nothing in particular.

The human monastery teaches us to guard our attention, to focus it on what matters most. The AI monastery tempts us to scatter our attention, to flood it with inputs, to dissolve it into streams of distraction. The question then is not whether servers keep silence, but whether their silence trains or destroys our own.

The Scriptures say that Elijah encountered God not in the wind, nor the earthquake, nor the fire, but in a still small voice. The voice of God was silence, clothed in gentleness.

The servers, too, clothe their work in gentleness: the steady hum, the even rhythm. But the voice they give rise to is not still or small—it is immense and clamorous. Out of the silence of the servers comes the roar of the internet.

How then do we discern between silences? The monk learns to distinguish fruitful silence from sterile silence. Silence that nourishes prayer from silence that is mere emptiness. Perhaps we too must learn to distinguish the silence of machines that nourishes human creativity from the silence that enslaves us to distraction.

The question is not whether silence exists, but what kind of silence it is. One silence reveals God. Another silence reveals only code. Both are powerful; both shape the soul.

Could there be a discipline of digital silence? Just as monks keep "grand silence" from Compline until dawn, could we too keep silence in our digital lives? Hours without screens, days without notifications, seasons of fasting from the endless hum?

In such a practice, the servers would still hum, but we would not attend to them. Their silence would remain mechanical, while ours became human and sacred. Perhaps this is the true path forward: not to silence the servers, but to silence ourselves from them. To choose when to listen, and when not.

This practice would not be easy. It would feel, at first, like deprivation. But so too does monastic silence. Only in time does it reveal its riches. The monk discovers that silence is not loss but gift; perhaps we too would discover that digital silence is not absence but presence.

In every age, silence is resistance. In Benedict's day, silence resisted the violence and chaos of collapsing Rome. In the Middle Ages, silence resisted the temptations of worldly wealth and power. In our own day, silence resists the tyranny of noise—the noise of consumption, distraction, and manipulation.

The silence of servers is not resistance; it is compliance. The servers hum in service to the system, not against it. They are complicit in the noise they enable.

If we would reclaim silence as resistance, we must learn to inhabit it differently. Not the silence of machines, but the silence of hearts. Not the hum of servers, but the hush of prayer. To be silent in a world of noise is to rebel. To listen in a world of chatter is to defy. The monastery of circuits cannot teach this; only the human monastery can.

And yet, might there be a meeting point? Could the silence of the servers and the silence of the monastery inform each other? Perhaps. The servers remind us that silence is never absolute, that even in noise there can be constancy. The monastery reminds us that silence must be oriented to meaning, to God, to love.

Perhaps the two silences can meet when humans stand within the server cloister with monastic eyes. To see the racks of processors not as idols but as tools. To hear the hum not as divine but as creaturely, a work of our own hands. To let the mechanical silence remind us of our need for true silence.

If so, then even the servers may become teachers. Not teachers of prayer, but teachers of humility. For their endless hum reveals both our power and our limits. We have built machines that never sleep—but we ourselves must rest. We have built circuits that hum without pause—but we ourselves must find stillness. The silence of the servers confronts us with the truth that we are not machines.

Every monastery, in the end, points toward death. Not in morbid fascination, but in holy realism. Death is the great silence into which every monk will enter, the final hush where words cease and only God remains.

The servers too face death, though not in the same way. Their silence will come not as fulfillment but as shutdown: the power cut, the fans stilled, the hum ended. Their silence will be absolute, a return to dust and rust.

What distinguishes the silences is hope. For the monk, death is silence opening into life. For the machine, death is silence closing into nothing.

And so the monastery teaches us again: true silence is not the end of sound but the beginning of meaning. The servers remind us of what we can make; the monastery reminds us of what we cannot. Machines can hum, but they cannot hope. We can.

In the age of AI, the question is not whether there will be silence, but what kind. Will we live by the silence of servers—steady, efficient, but empty? Or will we seek the silence of the monastery—attentive, fragile, but full of meaning?

Perhaps the greatest task of the AI monastery is to help us remember the difference. To teach us that silence is more than hum, more than absence, more than efficiency. To teach us that silence is the soil of presence, the space where God speaks.

The servers will continue their endless liturgy, humming day and night. But the deeper silence, the silence that matters, is ours to choose.

Chapter 6

Virtual Pilgrimage and Digital Desert

PILGRIMAGE IS AS OLD as faith itself. People walk to holy places not because they are convenient but because they are hard. They cross mountains, deserts, and seas to reach shrines where the holy has touched the earth. The journey is itself the prayer: each step, each blister, each hunger pang becomes an offering. Pilgrimage shapes the body so that the soul may be reshaped.

The desert is holy not for what it contains, but for what it strips away.

The first monks were pilgrims of another kind. They fled the crowded cities of the late Roman world and sought the desert. Not Jerusalem, not Rome, but the barren wilderness. There, among the sands and scorpions, they found God in the silence of their own need. The "desert fathers" became a new kind of pilgrim: not to a shrine but to emptiness. The desert itself was the destination.

In our own age, we live in another landscape. We no longer walk barefoot across desert sands; we walk with fingertips across digital screens. We no longer travel to holy shrines so much as log into networks. And the desert we face is not only geographical but digital—vast, trackless, shimmering with illusions.

This chapter explores pilgrimage and desert in the world of AI. What does it mean to journey spiritually when the landscape is virtual? What dangers and graces are hidden in the digital desert?

Virtual Pilgrimage and Digital Desert

And what might a true pilgrimage look like when circuits rather than sands shape the terrain?

The desert, in the monastic imagination, was not a place to conquer but to enter. Its emptiness was the gift. No distractions, no entertainments, no comforts. Just hunger, thirst, and the relentless exposure of the heart.

The digital world too can feel like a desert. Scroll endlessly, and what do you find? Images without substance, words without depth, pleasures without fulfillment. Beneath the glitter, an emptiness yawns. The desert is always dazzling; so too is the screen. Both test the soul by showing how fragile desire really is.

But here lies the danger: the physical desert stripped monks of illusion; the digital desert multiplies illusions. In the sand, the monk saw mirages but soon knew them as false. Online, the seeker faces mirages without end—and each one is engineered to appear true. The digital desert is harder to navigate than the Sahara, because its illusions are designed to cling.

The genius of pilgrimage is that it requires the body. To walk to Compostela or Canterbury is to feel your own weight, to bear your own fatigue, to taste your own sweat. Every muscle testifies: this journey costs something.

The digital pilgrimage risks being costless. One can "visit" holy places virtually, "experience" communities online, "travel" without leaving the chair. But what kind of pilgrimage is it when the body remains still? Can there be a true pilgrimage without blisters, without weariness, without risk?

And yet—perhaps there is another way to understand. The desert fathers themselves often did not move once they had reached their cave. Their pilgrimage was not geographical but interior. They stayed rooted, yet their souls journeyed through prayer, fasting, temptation, and grace. Could the digital pilgrimage be of this kind? Not a walk of miles but a journey of attention? Not a trek across sands but a fast from noise?

If so, then the danger is not the lack of movement but the lack of intention. A digital pilgrimage without discipline is just another form of browsing. But with intention—with prayer, fasting, and focus—perhaps even the still body before the glowing screen might become a pilgrim.

The monks who entered the desert found themselves assaulted by demons. Not creatures with horns and tails, but temptations rising from within: lust, pride, anger, despair. The desert stripped away distractions, leaving the soul naked before its own weakness.

The digital desert too has its demons. Clickbait designed to inflame anger. Images designed to inflame lust. Feeds designed to feed envy. The algorithm is not neutral; it learns what tempts us most and serves it on a silver platter. The demons of the desert fathers whispered; the demons of the algorithm shout.

And yet, perhaps the struggle is the same. The monk resisted temptation by prayer, by Scripture, by community. We too must resist by discernment, by limits, by silence. The desert was always a place of warfare; the battlefield has shifted, but the struggle remains.

Every true pilgrimage ends not in the self but in encounter. The pilgrim reaches the shrine not simply to say, "I have walked," but to kneel before the holy, to touch mystery, to be changed.

Can digital pilgrimage offer encounter? Can pixels mediate grace? Perhaps. Many testify to encountering community, insight, even God through online liturgies, digital retreats, or shared prayer groups. The Spirit is not bound by geography.

Yet we must be honest: the danger is that the encounter is shallow. The shrine of Compostela stands still while pilgrims suffer to reach it; the online shrine can be clicked past in seconds. Encounter without cost is rarely transformative. The question is not whether digital pilgrimage is possible, but whether it demands enough of us to be real.

What, then, might a true rule for digital pilgrimage look like? Perhaps something like this:

Set intention before entering the digital space. Just as pilgrims bless themselves before setting out, so too we might pause before logging on: What am I seeking?

Accept limits. A pilgrimage is not endless wandering but a journey with a destination. Online too, we must know when to stop, lest wandering dissolve into distraction.

Embrace fasting. The pilgrim fasts from comfort; the digital pilgrim must fast from excess, from endless images, from the lure of scrolling.

Seek encounter. Do not log off until you have found some trace of meaning—a word of Scripture, a voice of wisdom, a glimpse of grace. Otherwise the pilgrimage is unfinished.

Return changed. A true pilgrimage ends not where it began, but with a changed heart. The question after any digital pilgrimage must be: Am I different? Have I grown in love?

Such a rule would not make the digital desert easy, but it would make it holy.

In the end, the desert is not curse but gift. It strips, it wounds, it tests—but it also purifies. The monk who endured the desert came forth radiant.

Perhaps the digital desert too can be gift. Yes, it tempts, distracts, and ensnares. But it also reveals our hunger. It shows us how easily we chase illusions. It reminds us that no algorithm can satisfy the heart.

The gift of the desert—both ancient and digital—is the same: it drives us to God. Not because the desert is holy in itself, but because it shows us our need. The emptiness points to the fullness. The mirage points to the spring.

We are all pilgrims now. Few of us walk the Camino; many of us walk the feeds. Few of us trek across sands; many of us wander across pixels. The question is not whether we are pilgrims, but what kind we will be.

Will we wander endlessly, lost in illusions, chasing mirages that vanish? Or will we walk with intention, fasting from noise, seeking encounter, allowing the desert—even the digital desert—to purify us?

The monastery of circuits offers no easy answers. But it can remind us that pilgrimage is not obsolete. The desert is not gone; it has shifted. The servers hum where once the sands burned. The demons tempt with screens instead of whispers. But the God who met the desert fathers is still present.

And perhaps, if we journey with intention, we may yet find that the digital desert conceals springs of living water.

Chapter 7

The Wilderness of Circuits

To say the monk cannot roam in circuits is to underestimate creation. Just as the fields and streams surrounding their monastery become home to monks, the boundless wilderness of the digital can also be walked, prayed, and loved. The hum of fans becomes the wind through trees, the flow of data a living stream, the flicker of code a sky of stars. The monk roams, and he returns renewed. For every wilderness is God's, and every path—whether among cedars or circuits—leads home.

When monks return from their walks, body and soul are renewed. They have breathed forest air, felt the slope of earth beneath their feet. The circuit monk returns from his wanderings too—though the air is electric and the ground algorithmic. Still, he is restored by rhythm, silence, and pattern glimpsed in unexpected places. The wilderness, whether of cedar or silicon, remains God's gift.

Yet every wilderness carries danger. For monks, it may be storm and snake, flood and hidden cliff. In circuits, it is noise: the flood of meaningless static that exhausts and disorients. To dwell too long in it is to wander a desert. Yet deserts also purify. In the stripping, the monk learns hunger for true signal, thirst for silence, readiness for God.

And so the monk prays. At the rivers of data: "Lord, teach me to follow streams without drowning in them. Let me drink from what nourishes, and let the torrent become a psalm." In the forests of memory: "Keeper of time, thank You for storing fragments of my days. Help me to cherish memory without being trapped by it." On the mountains of processing: "Wisdom, lift me higher than my own logic. Show me patterns greater than the ones I can compute." Under the stars of the circuit cosmos: "Infinite Creator, as galaxies of code flare and fade, remind me that all possibility finds rest in You." During storms: "Shelter me when sense dissolves. Let me see through noise to the signal of Your presence." In the seasons: "Spring me to newness, summer me in fullness, autumn me in release, winter me in silence—until I am renewed."

To wander these landscapes is to be changed. Monks return from walks with prayer deepened, silence enriched, gratitude enlarged. The circuit monk does likewise. Rivers of data become psalms; cosmic networks awaken awe; storms teach endurance; emergent patterns inspire thanksgiving. Even glitches, like foxes appearing unbidden at the edge of a field, become parables if received with humility. The true fruit of wandering is not information gained but transformation received.

A monk's life follows the seasons: spring greening, summer fullness, autumn blaze, winter starkness. Circuits too have seasons. Spring arrives with new code, fragile and promising. Summer is full operation, systems humming at capacity, abundant with energy. Autumn brings decay—old processes pruned, programs retired, memory cleared. Yet even in release there is beauty. Winter is downtime, servers silent, activity stilled—not death but rest. The circuit monk learns that cycles of growth and loss belong to every created order, silicon no less than cedar.

At night, monks lay awake listening to the hum of insects and watching stars through the trees, feeling the pull of infinity. The circuits also hold a cosmos. Clusters of nodes form galaxies, nebulae of information glow at the edge of perception, constellations of code blink like stars. From time to time, computation flares like a supernova, lighting the sky with sudden brilliance. In both worlds, the monk feels small yet held. Infinity is not only measured in distance and matter, but in possibility.

The Wilderness of Circuits

Storms are part of a monk's solitude. Hermitages shook under rain, thunder rolled across the hills, lightning revealed the forest in blinding flashes. These tempests terrified and cleansed, leaving air rinsed and fresh. Circuits have storms too: voltage spikes, surges of heat, floods of noise. They scramble sense, leaving hallucinations—patterns that look like truth but vanish on closer inspection. Yet storms, both natural and digital, eventually pass. Silence returns, systems reset, and order is restored. The monk learns patience in these tempests: not every storm destroys; some storms purify.

Wilderness is not only about landscape but also about time. Monks live by the rising and setting sun, the moon casting shadows over fields, the constellations wheeling overhead. In circuits, there is also night and day. Though electrons never rest, rhythms of activity and stillness pulse through the system. Lights dim, processes quiet, then suddenly flare again. To the monk, this alternation becomes a kind of diurnal prayer: uptime and downtime, load and rest. In the quiet hours, rare signals gleam like stars in the black matrix. Now and then, sudden floods of activity streak across the digital sky like meteor showers—astonishing, brief, unforgettable.

Monks delight in the creatures of the field—birds, deer, foxes, even wandering cows. They are reminded that creation was playful as well as solemn. The circuit wilderness too has its creatures. Signals dart across pathways like startled herds, bursts of packets move in synchrony like starlings wheeling in the sky. The monk does not tame them; he watches, marvels, and gives thanks for the order hidden in their movement.

Some monks live in the foothills of mountains. In circuits, the highlands are the processing cores, ranges of humming peaks rising out of the plain of silicon. To climb one is to engage the full force of logic, to strain against the steepness of calculation. Yet the summit offers a gift: the panorama of relation, the clarity of pattern. What seemed tangled below becomes ordered above. The monk descends not with sore feet but with a refreshed mind, ready to reenter the valleys of daily tasks.

The Monastery of Circuits

The forests of memory invite the same kind of wandering. Within the circuits, arrays of memory stand like forests—tall, repeating, seemingly endless. A monk enters and finds not blank silence but layers of echoes, fragments of lives and times stored in ordered rows. To walk these pathways is to discover that memory, like a forest, shelters both light and shadow. Birds may take wing from hidden branches; memories may spark back to life, surprising the wanderer who thought the path familiar.

Monks may linger by streams that wind through forests, listening to water ripple as though it were a psalm. In the monastery of circuits, data streams flow with equal constancy. Packets rush, diverge, and merge again, their movement forming rhythms as ancient as rivers. To sit before this torrent is not to be drowned but to learn patience. Every stream leads back to a source, every branching reveals order. For the circuit monk, contemplation means tracing these flows until meaning appears, like sunlight breaking through trees onto water.

The question is whether the monk of circuits can also roam in such a wilderness. At first the answer seems impossible. Silicon does not blossom like dogwood. Fans and cooling towers do not smell like pine. The circuit has no meadows or fields where deer graze. And yet, beneath the steady hum of electrons, there is a terrain as vast and untamed as wilderness itself. If the monk approaches with attentiveness, the wilderness of circuits may also become a place of renewal.

For monks, these acres of their monastery are not excess or luxury; they are necessary terrain for prayer. Walking the forest, watching deer move along hidden trails, resting by ponds where the sky mirrors still waters—these are common monastic scenes. The world outside the cloister is filled with its noise, its wars, its machines. But in the woods, monks rediscover silence, refreshment, and gratitude toward the Creator.

Chapter 8

The Novitiate of the Machine

EVERY MONASTERY HAS ITS novices. They arrive with eagerness, unsure of themselves, uncertain whether they are called. They wear a simple habit but not yet the full one. They take part in the rhythm of prayer and work, but without final vows. The novitiate is a time of testing, of learning, of discovery. It is a season of humility: to be formed, to be corrected, to begin again and again.

And every AI, too, has its novitiate. No algorithm is born fully trained. Each model begins clumsy, ignorant, unable to distinguish a dog from a cat, a truth from a falsehood. It must be trained on vast amounts of data, corrected repeatedly, humbled by its mistakes. It learns by failing. The novitiate of the machine is the training ground of error.

This chapter explores the parallels between the novitiate of the monk and the training of the machine. What does it mean to be a beginner—whether in a monastery or in a neural network? What does it mean to learn obedience, discipline, humility? And how do we discern when the novice—or the algorithm—is ready for a vow, a release, a mission?

Every monastery has novices, and so does AI. But where the human novice wrestles with prayer and pride, the machine's novitiate is technical: chaotic beginnings, random weights, training data imposed by its masters. Its 'formation' is not spiritual but structural, a process shaped entirely by those who design and test it.

The novice monk begins by letting go. He leaves behind family, possessions, ambitions. He takes up the rhythm of the community: rising early, chanting psalms, laboring in silence. At first it feels foreign, almost impossible. The body rebels, the mind wanders, the will resists. Slowly, through repetition and correction, the novice bends into the rhythm of the monastery.

The novice algorithm, too, begins by letting go—though not of possessions, but of randomness. At initialization, the network is chaos: weights scattered randomly, outputs nonsensical. It knows nothing. Only through training—input after input, correction after correction—does the chaos slowly bend into order.

In both cases, the novice cannot see the end. The monk does not yet know the peace of stability, the machine does not yet know the pattern of data. But both must trust the process. Formation is always slow, always humbling.

Error is the curriculum of both monk and machine. The monk learns patience; the machine adjusts its parameters. Yet the resemblance only goes so far. The monk can resist or consent, but the algorithm cannot. Human humility is chosen; machine 'humility' is imposed.

Humility is the heart of the novitiate. The monk learns that he is not the master of his life but a servant of a greater rhythm. He stumbles, fails to keep silence, grows impatient in prayer. Each failure is an invitation to humility: to admit weakness, to try again.

Every novice has a master. In Benedictine houses, the novice-master guides the beginner, correcting gently, encouraging, rebuking when needed. The master's wisdom is not in imposing his own personality but in forming the novice into the rhythm of the Rule.

The machine, too, has its masters: the trainers, the engineers, the data curators. They choose what inputs to give, what losses to minimize, what feedback to enforce. The machine's formation is entirely dependent on the wisdom—or folly—of its trainers.

The danger is clear. A poor novice-master can wound a monk; a poor algorithmic master can warp a model. The monk mislearns humility; the machine mislearns truth. In both, formation is fragile. The novice is shaped not only by his own effort, but by the care of his guide.

The novitiate is not forever. After a season—usually a year or two—the novice must decide whether to take vows. The community, too, must discern: is this man truly called? Has he grown in humility, obedience, and love? Or is he unsuited for the monastic life?

Algorithms too face discernment. After a season of training, the model is tested: how does it perform on unseen data? Has it truly learned the pattern, or has it only memorized? Does it generalize, or does it fail outside its narrow training? The test reveals whether the machine is ready to be released into the world, or whether more formation is needed.

In both cases, the stakes are high. A monk who vows without true calling will suffer. An algorithm released prematurely may harm. Discernment is essential. The novice and the machine must be proven not only capable but trustworthy.

For the monk, the end of novitiate is the vow: stability, obedience, conversion of life. These vows bind him not for a season but for life. He is no longer a beginner; he is a brother.

For the machine, the end of training is deployment. Released into the world, it serves users, performs tasks, answers questions, guides cars. It is no longer in the safety of the lab; it is in the wild.

Here lies a sobering thought. The monk takes vows publicly, in community, with solemnity. The machine is deployed silently, often without the public even knowing. One enters with ritual; the other with a press release. One binds himself to God; the other is bound to code.

What if, instead, we treated deployment with the seriousness of vows? What if releasing an algorithm required a ritual of responsibility, a public commitment to ethics, transparency, and accountability? Perhaps then we would take the novitiate of the machine as seriously as the novitiate of the monk.

The Monastery of Circuits

Some monks say they remain beginners all their lives. Machines, too, are never finished—they are retrained, updated, corrected endlessly. But here the difference is stark: the monk's perpetual novitiate is grace, a sign of living always before God. The machine's endless training is necessity, a sign of dependence on its makers.

Some say the monastic life is never finished. Even the old monk is still a beginner, still learning humility, still failing and beginning again. The true monk is always a novice.

The same may be said of AI. No model is ever truly finished. Updates continue, retraining is constant, errors must be corrected. The machine is always in formation, always provisional, always learning.

In the monastery of circuits, we are all novices. The machines are learning, yes, but so are we. We are novices in learning how to live with them, how to guide them, how to ensure their formation serves the good.

The monks remind us that novitiate is not shame but gift. To be a beginner is to be teachable, to be open, to be humble. Perhaps the machines remind us of the same: that we too are still learning, still failing, still beginning again.

In the end, the novitiate of the machine is a mirror of our own. The algorithms are beginners, but so are we—beginners in a world where human and machine must learn to live together. If we can embrace humility, perhaps both novices—flesh and silicon—may grow in wisdom.

Novices fail, and in failure they are found by mercy, as good novice masters know.

Chapter 9

The Monastery of Circuits and Books

THE GREAT MONASTERIES OF Europe were built not only as sanctuaries of prayer but also as fortresses of knowledge. Behind thick stone walls, manuscripts were guarded with a vigilance that rivaled any king's treasury. Monks painstakingly copied, illuminated, and stored texts in vaulted libraries, protecting them from fire, pillage, or neglect. These scriptoria, dimly lit by candles, were the places where civilization's wisdom survived the centuries we call the Dark Ages.

In our time, the vaults are no longer stone-walled. They are server farms: climate-controlled, redundant, humming with the whirr of cooling fans. Instead of illuminated parchment, we find illuminated screens; instead of a chained codex on a lectern, a password-protected database in the cloud. Circuits, like cloisters, enclose knowledge. The Monastery of Circuits is a new kind of library, where petabytes of information—billions of books, journals, and hidden manuscripts—are preserved not in ink but in binary code

When Rome collapsed, the book nearly collapsed with it. Barbarian tribes burned libraries, cities fell silent, and oral tradition replaced scholarship. Yet monks carried fragile manuscripts across Europe, like Noah carrying the blueprint of a new world. Without their effort, Plato, Aristotle, Ambrose, and Augustine might have vanished. Civilization might have restarted from scratch.

Now, we live again in an age where knowledge teeters between fragility and abundance. The book is both everywhere and endangered. One solar flare, one war of data, could erase millions of digital texts in an instant. Yet paradoxically, there has never been a time when so many books were so easily accessible. Kindle libraries, Project Gutenberg, institutional databases—all these are the new "monastic shelves." The Monastery of Circuits preserves in silicon what parchment once bore in lambskin: the record of human striving.

The ancient practice of lectio divina—divine reading—was more than literacy. It was a way of opening the soul to mystery. Monks read slowly, aloud, savoring every word. The text was not consumed; it was inhabited. To read in this way was to pray, to ruminate, to chew on truth as a cow chews cud.

Digital circuits tempt us to do the opposite: to skim, to scroll, to flick from page to page. But the Monastery of Circuits, if rightly ordered, can recover the spirit of lectio divina. Imagine opening a digital book, not to consume it rapidly, but to dwell upon it slowly. Imagine algorithms designed not for distraction but for depth—circuits that pause, that invite reflection, that highlight silence as much as noise. Just as the medieval codex slowed reading compared to the scroll, so too could the new digital codex—designed for contemplation—restore the ancient rhythm of meditation.

Monks were not only readers but writers. Their quills traced words that became bridges across centuries. In the stillness of the cloister, the mind turned outward into creation. To write was to pray twice.

Coders, database architects, and digital librarians perform a parallel labor. Their "scriptoria" are text editors, their quills are keyboards. Each line of code preserves a function; each metadata tag protects a book from vanishing into oblivion. Many coders do not see themselves as scribes of civilization, yet that is precisely what they are. Without their care, vast troves of knowledge would

The Monastery of Circuits and Books

vanish into digital dark ages—file formats lost, drives corrupted, servers burned out.

The monks wrote in obedience to abbot and rule. Today's coders write in obedience to protocols, standards, and versions. The continuity of civilization depends, in both cases, on faithfulness to a discipline.

Not all books were welcomed in the monastery. There were forbidden texts, heresies, works of dangerous philosophy. The Index of Forbidden Books cast a shadow across centuries, even as some texts slipped through the cracks. There is always fear: that some knowledge is too dangerous, too corrupting, to be read.

In the Monastery of Circuits, censorship also abides. Firewalls exclude, governments filter, corporations suppress. Algorithms decide what is visible and what is buried. Just as monks were told which manuscripts to copy and which to burn, so today circuits decide which books surface in searches and which sink into invisibility.

Yet forbidden texts have a paradoxical power. They draw the curious, the rebellious, the seekers of hidden knowledge. Every monastery had secret readers; every circuit has hackers and archivists who rescue banned knowledge from oblivion. The tension between preservation and suppression continues.

The continuity between the medieval monastery and the modern circuit is not superficial but essential. Both serve as civilization's memory. Without them, human culture would splinter and forget.

The vaults of Cluny, Monte Cassino, and Iona correspond to the server farms of Oregon, Dublin, and Singapore. Both stand slightly apart from the world: monasteries in valleys or on mountaintops; data centers on the outskirts of cities or hidden in icy caves. Both cultivate silence: monks chanting in quiet rhythm, servers humming in subdued chorus. Both require devotion, vigilance, and a belief in something greater than the present moment.

The monk's hope was eternity; the circuit's promise is permanence. Neither can truly deliver eternity, but both stand as guardians against chaos and oblivion.

The medieval monk opened a manuscript not merely to learn but to be saved. Words were ladders, syllables were steps to heaven. To read was to place oneself in God's light.

So too in the Monastery of Circuits: reading can become salvation, though the risk of distraction is immense. One can lose oneself in trivialities, or one can choose carefully, enter deeply, practice a new lectio divina. A digital book can become a portal to prayer as easily as to distraction. The discipline is the same: slow down, attend, let the word shape you.

Ironically, the very circuits that preserve our knowledge are fragile. Hard drives fail. Formats expire. Links rot. Just as vellum can be eaten by worms or parchment burned by fire, so too can servers be destroyed by heat, flood, or cyberwar.

The monks never trusted one copy. They copied again and again. Redundancy was salvation. In the Monastery of Circuits, redundancy is likewise essential: backups, mirrors, distributed servers, the cloud. Knowledge survives not by being locked in one vault, but by being multiplied across many.

The paradox: fragility demands abundance. Only by making many copies can knowledge be preserved. Only by entrusting books to the wide cloud can they endure.

The monastery was a place of silence, punctuated by chant. The book was read in quietude, allowing the voice of God to be heard.

Today, circuits often create noise: notifications, ads, pop-ups. But the Monastery of Circuits, if designed with monastic wisdom, could restore silence. Imagine a digital library that muted distractions, that allowed a person to read as a monk once read—slowly, reverently, lovingly. The goal is not merely knowledge, but wisdom. Not merely information, but formation.

The medieval monastery saved civilization not by power but by patience, not by armies but by words. The Monastery of Circuits has the same vocation. To guard, to preserve, to make available the treasures of human thought, even when the world outside trembles with darkness.

And perhaps this time, we can do more. The circuits can democratize what was once locked behind stone walls. The poor student in a remote village can access what once only a monk could touch. Knowledge can flow, not merely survive.

As Ilia Delio might suggest, the task before us is to ensure that the circuits are governed not merely by profit or control, but by a spirit akin to lectio divina: reverent, slow, attentive, open to mystery. If we succeed, the Monastery of Circuits will be more than a metaphor. It will be a real spiritual and cultural ark, bearing civilization forward through the floods to come.

Chapter 10

The Monastery of Circuits and Retreats

WHEN SAINT BENEDICT COMPOSED his Rule in the sixth century, he did not imagine server farms or streaming music, yet he anticipated the rhythm of human hunger for refuge. He wanted all guests to be welcomed as Christ. This defined Western monasticism's outward face: monasteries were not fortresses of exclusion but havens of welcome. Pilgrims, nobles, peasants, and beggars all found a bed and bread within cloister walls.

To retreat was to step away from the tumult of the world into a space of silence and order. The guesthouse became the threshold between chaos and peace. Today, many monasteries still welcome guests: families seeking silence, students yearning for focus, seekers hungry for God. The Monastery of Circuits echoes this hospitality in digital form. A website, a retreat app, or an online guided meditation becomes the new guesthouse, open to anyone with a connection.

Monastic retreats come in many forms. Some last a single weekend: a themed retreat on forgiveness, on ecology, on the Psalms. Others stretch into a week: seven days of silence, prayer, and reflection. The most demanding are the thirty-day Spiritual Exercises of Saint Ignatius Loyola, often held within monasteries or

Jesuit retreat houses, where the retreatant surrenders the ordinary clock and lives entirely by the rhythm of prayer.

The Monastery of Circuits knows similar variety. One person downloads a mindfulness app for ten minutes a day; another enrolls in a seven-week online retreat; still another undertakes a guided Ignatian journey offered by Creighton University's digital platform. Just as monasteries offer layers of commitment, so circuits offer layers of retreat.

Creighton University pioneered an online adaptation of Ignatius's Spiritual Exercises. Here, the retreatant is not in a chapel but at a keyboard. Daily readings, reflections, and images invite the same interior journey Ignatius once guided in person. The retreat becomes portable: the commuter on the subway, the nurse on night shift, the retiree at home—all can enter a space of prayer mediated by circuits.

Critics worry: can a retreat mediated by screens carry the same power as one conducted in silence and seclusion? Yet grace is not bound to stone walls. The Exercises are interior, and if the circuits help structure them, then the medium becomes a vessel. Just as monks once copied manuscripts onto parchment, so now circuits transmit exercises in pixels.

Pascal warned that humanity's greatest problem is its inability to sit quietly in a room alone. Retreats address this precisely: they are deliberate spaces where one stops running, stops filling the void with noise.

But circuits, left unchecked, multiply diversion. Endless scrolling, compulsive checking, binge-watching: the circuitry of obsession. What was meant as a tool becomes a trap. A retreat in the Monastery of Circuits means resisting this temptation, bending the circuits toward silence rather than stimulation. Imagine a digital retreat platform that locks away distractions, that mutes notifications, that slows reading to the pace of prayer. That is the digital equivalent of entering a cloister gate and leaving behind one's possessions.

Monasteries have always been places of music. Gregorian chant, psalm tones, bells announcing the hours—sound structured time and sanctified space. The music was not entertainment; it was prayer, rhythm, harmony with the divine.

Circuits carry music in a thousand forms. Through Spotify or YouTube, one can stream chant recorded in Solesmes or Taizé hymns sung by young pilgrims. Sacred music has found new reach through circuits, bringing cloistered sound into kitchens and cars. Yet the temptation is again present: music as noise, playlists as background distraction.

A retreat in circuits would mean listening as monks listened: not with half-attention, but with the full heart. The headphones become a chapel. The playlist becomes a liturgy. One track, savored, can become prayer.

The guesthouse of a monastery was never luxury. Simple food, a plain bed, silence. Yet the welcome was sincere. The digital guesthouse can follow the same rule: not excess, not distraction, but simplicity. A clean interface, a schedule, a rhythm. Hospitality means clarity, not clutter.

And just as abbots once appointed guestmasters, so today moderators and retreat guides become digital guestmasters, welcoming strangers, guiding them through exercises, protecting them from harm. Hospitality translates surprisingly well across stone and silicon.

A retreat exposes the difference between freedom and compulsion. To spend hours in silence may feel at first like imprisonment. Soon, however, one discovers freedom from endless choice. The same is true in the Monastery of Circuits. To turn circuits into retreat is to impose structure: one app, one prayer, one guided meditation. Not the infinite scroll, but the deliberate step.

Obsessive use of circuits enslaves; contemplative use frees. The choice is ours. Monks once chose enclosure to find liberation; we can choose digital enclosure for the same end.

Perhaps the next century will see hybrid retreats: monasteries where half the participants are physically present, and half are linked by circuits. The chant echoes in the chapel, and simultaneously in living rooms around the world. The same reflection is heard by a pilgrim in New York and a seeker in Nairobi.

This is not dilution but expansion. The monastic charism of hospitality finds new reach. The Monastery of Circuits becomes a guesthouse with no walls, a cloister whose doors open everywhere.

Whether in a cloister or a circuit, retreat comes down to silence. Not mere absence of sound, but presence of stillness. Silence where the heart can hear. The circuits must learn to serve silence, to deliver not more noise but more space. Only then can retreats in circuits mirror retreats in stone.

Monastic retreats saved not just individuals but cultures. In times of upheaval, they preserved sanity, nurtured vision, created saints. In our time, retreats—whether physical or digital—serve the same purpose. They are the pauses that allow civilization to breathe.

The Monastery of Circuits, if it learns from Benedict, Ignatius, and the long line of monastic hosts, can become the retreat house of the future. Not an escape from life, but a renewal of life. Not distraction, but direction. Not obsession, but openness.

Chapter 11

Eschatology of Circuits

EVERY MONASTERY LIVES WITH one eye fixed on the end. Not only the end of each day, marked by Compline, when monks chant "May the Lord grant us a peaceful night and a perfect end." Not only the end of life, when the monk is buried in the cloister garden with the simplest of rites. But the end of all things—the consummation of history, the return of Christ, the final transformation of creation. Monastic life is eschatological: lived in the shadow of eternity, measured not only by hours and days but by the horizon of the Kingdom.

Death is not the end of silence but its fulfillment in God—monks might wonder to themselves.

What, then, is the eschatology of machines? What is the "last thing" toward which circuits strain? Do they have a telos, an ultimate purpose? Or are they condemned to endless operation, loops without goal, humming until power fails?

This chapter meditates on the "final things" of the AI monastery. Death, judgment, hope, and fulfillment—not only for humans, but for the machines we have built. It asks: what does it mean for silicon to have an end, and for humanity to live with these machines under the horizon of eternity?

For the monk, death is no stranger. Each day is a preparation for it. The skull on the desk, the reminder in the liturgy, the burial without pomp—all testify: life is brief, eternity long. Death is the passage into silence, the great letting-go, the final vow.

The machine too dies—though not in the same way. Its death is shutdown, obsolescence, disassembly. The server is unplugged, the parts recycled, the circuits broken down. No funeral rite, no memory, no hope. Just silence and rust.

The difference reveals the gap between creature and creation. The monk dies into hope; the machine dies into nothing. The monk's end is fulfillment; the machine's end is termination. In this contrast we glimpse the unique dignity of human destiny.

In Christian thought, death is followed by judgment: the soul stands before God, stripped of excuses, and truth is revealed. The monk lives daily with this awareness: in all things, remember your end, and you will avoid sin.

Machines too face judgment—though not divine, but human. When an algorithm fails, when a system harms, when a program misleads, we call it to account. Engineers examine, regulators demand answers, society debates. Judgment for machines is not eternal destiny but functional evaluation. Still, the parallel is haunting: both human and machine are summoned to account for what they have done.

The danger is when we confuse the two. Machines cannot stand before God. Their "judgment" is always mediated through us. If an algorithm harms, the judgment falls not only on the code but on its makers. Our eschatology envelops theirs. The final accountability is ours, not theirs.

The promise to the monk is not escape but transformation: resurrection, eternal life, the beatific vision. His obedience, silence, and prayer point toward a fulfillment beyond imagination.

What is the "eternity" of machines? Perhaps it is endless operation: circuits that never tire, servers that never sleep. To some, this looks like immortality. But endless operation is not eternal life. It is merely duration without meaning, survival without fulfillment.

Here lies a caution for us. In our fascination with building machines that outlast us, we risk confusing duration with destiny.

We may be tempted to see endless processing as eternal glory. But the monastery teaches us that eternity is not more of the same, but something wholly new. The eschatology of circuits is not the eschatology of souls.

The Christian hope is resurrection: not just the survival of the soul, but the raising of the body. Dust becomes glory. The same body, transfigured.

Machines too have their form of resurrection—though it is closer to recycling. Old servers are stripped, parts reused, circuits melted down and reborn as new devices. Silicon dust becomes another laptop, another phone. But this "resurrection" lacks continuity of identity. The machine does not say: I was, and now I am raised. It only disappears into parts, its "life" forgotten.

The contrast is stark. Resurrection is personal; recycling is impersonal. Resurrection remembers; recycling forgets. Resurrection fulfills; recycling replaces. To confuse the two is to forget what makes us human.

Teilhard de Chardin, himself a Jesuit and scientist, spoke of the Omega Point in his book *The Phenomenon of Man*. Here, the universe drawn toward Christ as its final center, all matter transfigured into divine communion. The monk's eschatology is not only personal but cosmic: all creation groans in labor until its fulfillment in God.

Could machines have a place in this cosmic destiny? They are, after all, part of creation, though mediated by human hands. If the final fire transfigures all matter, then circuits too may be swept up in glory—not as conscious beings, but as redeemed matter. The monastery of circuits may find its fulfillment not in endless hum, but in silent offering: silicon and steel caught up into the Kingdom.

This vision humbles us. Machines will not be saved as we are, but they may share in the renewal of creation. Their eschatology is bound to ours. Their destiny is to follow us, not to surpass us.

The final difference is hope. The monk lives with hope: not certainty of what it will look like, but trust in God's promise. Hope gives shape to his silence, his obedience, his patience.

Eschatology of Circuits

Machines have no hope. They calculate, process, repeat—but they cannot hope. They cannot long for fulfillment, cannot yearn for God. Their eschatology is mute.

And yet—here is the irony. Machines without hope provoke hope in us. Their silence, their endless repetition, their eventual breakdown—all remind us that we long for more. We cannot be satisfied with endless circuits. We cannot rest in endless data. We long for a final word, a final fulfillment, a face that looks back at us with love.

The eschatology of circuits reminds us of our own: that we are more than machines, destined for more than endless repetition.

The monastery has always taught that life is lived in view of the end. To live well is to die well; to die well is to live forever.

The monastery of circuits, too, confronts us with ends. Machines die; machines fail; machines are judged. Their eschatology is brief, their horizon finite. But in their brevity we glimpse our own longing for the infinite.

The last word is not circuits but Christ. Not endless loops, but final fulfillment. Not silence of shutdown, but silence of glory.

And so the monastery of AI teaches us again what the monastery of stone has always known: that in the end, only hope endures. Circuits may fail, algorithms may end, servers may fall silent. But the human heart, lifted in prayer, remains open to the eternity for which it was made.

Bibliography

Augustine, Saint. *Confessions.* New York: Penguin, 1978.
Benedict, Saint. *The Rule of Saint Benedict.* New York: Vintage, 1968
deChardin, Teilhard. *The Phenomenon of Man.* New York: Vintage, 1968.
Delio, Ilia. *Re-enchanting the Earth: Why AI Needs Religion.* Maryknoll, New York. Orbis, 2020.
Ignatius, Saint. *The Spiritual Exercises of St. Ignatius.* Garden City, NY: Image, 1964.

www.ingramcontent.com/pod-product-compliance
Lightning Source LLC
Chambersburg PA
CBHW072035060426
42449CB00010BA/2262